A Tige

by Maryellen Gregoire

Nancy E. Harris, M.Ed—Reading
National Reading Consultant

capstone
classroom
Heinemann Raintree • Red Brick Learning
division of Capstone

A cub can eat.

A cub can sit.

A cub can roll.

A cub can jump.

A cub can run.

A cub can hunt.

A cub can sleep.